EXPERIENCING SUCCESS

GOD'S WAY

BY

CHARLES F. STANLEY

THOMAS NELSON
Since 1798

NASHVILLE   DALLAS   MEXICO CITY   RIO DE JANEIRO

Editing, layout, and design by Gregory C. Benoit Publishing, Old Mystic, CT.

Unless otherwise noted, Scripture quotations are from the New King James Version. © 1982 by Thomas Nelson, Inc. Used by permission. All rights reserved.

ISBN 9781418541255

Printed in the United States of America

09 10 11 12 13 W C 5 4 3 2 1

Contents

Defining Success—God's Way

Countless books on success are on the market today. I've probably read enough of them to fill two or three bookshelves. Some of the authors have included God in their discussion of success, and a few have even put God at the center of a successful life. One thing that I've discovered in reading these books, however, is that, without exception, every genuine success principle that they describe can be found in the Bible. The principles of genuine success are not foreign to a godly life; they are embedded in a godly life. The world may think that it has discovered some new idea about success, but in truth God is the author of all success, and the Bible is the foremost "success book" you can ever read.

One of the key words that the Bible uses to describe success is *prosperity*. To prosper in all you do is to succeed in all you do. To be prosperous is to be successful. Any time we read in the Bible about the Lord prospering His people, we can be assured that the Lord is helping His people to succeed in all ways.

Another key concept related to Bible prosperity is *whole-person prosperity*. We read in 3 John 2, "Beloved, I pray that you may prosper in all things and be in health, just as your soul prospers." To prosper in all things is to prosper materially, socially, naturally, and financially—and also to prosper emotionally, spiritually, and in every creative endeavor. God wants the success principles of His Word to touch every aspect of your life—your spiritual walk, finances, vocation, service to the Lord, health, and relationships with family members and friends.

A third Bible concept about success is that we, as the Lord's followers, will prosper outwardly *as our souls prosper*. Inner prosperity and success and wholeness lead to outer prosperity, success, and wholeness. Many people approach success from the outside in. They look at the external trappings of success and conclude that a person surely must be experiencing inner peace, joy, hope, love, and faith. Not so. Genuine success begins on the inside and works its way out.

Most people are seeking to prosper in their finances and material lives with very little regard to their souls prospering. The challenge of the Bible is to place greater emphasis on the inner state of our prosperity than on the outer. The challenge is to grow spiritually, and as we do, the outer manifestations of prosperity will appear in the form of fruitfulness and blessing. Furthermore, the degree to which we prosper spiritually will be in direct proportion to the degree that we prosper materially, in our work, and in our relationships.

This book can be used by you alone or by several people in a small-group study. At various times, you will be asked to relate to the material in one of these four ways:

1. **What new insights have you gained?** Make notes about the insights that you have. You may want to record them in your Bible or in a separate journal. As you reflect back over your insights, you are likely to see how God has moved in your life.

2. **Have you ever had a similar experience?** Each of us approaches the Bible from a unique background—our own particular set of relationships and experiences. Our experiences do not make the Bible true—the Word of God is truth regardless of our opinion about it. It is important, however, to share our experiences in order to see how God's truth can be applied to human lives.

3. *How do you feel about the material presented?* Emotional responses do not give validity to the Scriptures, nor should we trust our emotions as a gauge for our faith. In small-group Bible study, however, it is good for participants to express their emotions. The Holy Spirit often communicates with us through this unspoken language.

4. *In what way do you feel challenged to respond or to act?* God's Word may cause you to feel inspired or challenged to change something in your life. Take the challenge seriously and find ways of acting upon it. If God reveals to you a particular need that He wants you to address, take that as "marching orders" from God. God is expecting you to do something with the challenge that He has just given you.

Start and conclude your Bible study sessions in prayer. Ask God to give you spiritual eyes to see and spiritual ears to hear. As you conclude your study, ask the Lord to seal what you have learned so that you will never forget it. Ask Him to help you grow into the fullness of the stature of Christ Jesus.

Again, I caution you to keep the Bible at the center of your study. A genuine Bible study stays focused on God's Word and promotes a growing faith and a closer walk with the Holy Spirit in each person who participates.

∾ **Notes and Prayer Requests:** ∾

LESSON 1

God Wants You to Succeed!

─────── ❧ **In This Lesson** ☙ ───────

LEARNING: WHAT EXACTLY IS SUCCESS?

GROWING: HOW DO I ATTAIN THAT SUCCESS?

"Some people are just born to be successful." "A Christian can't really be successful—too many worldly things are required if I am going to achieve success." "God is interested in many things, but my success isn't one of them." "I'm not sure that I can count on God to help me succeed in reaching my goals."

If you hold any of these attitudes, I want to share this good news with you. God does want you to be successful. He is deeply committed to your success, if you are willing to pursue success *His* way and to adopt *His* definition of success. And yes, Christians can be successful—including *you.*

Success does not belong only to those who are born with a certain degree of privilege or who achieve a basic level of education or social acceptance. Neither is success associated with lying, cheating, dishonesty, or other actions that are apart from God's commandments for Christian living. Rather, success is God's plan for Christians. Furthermore, most of the concepts that the world calls "principles for success" are actually based upon God's Word.

God's Definition of Success

At the very outset of this study guide, I believe it is important for us to define success from God's perspective and to compare that definition with the world's definition. From the world's perspective, success is subject to a great deal of individual interpretation. A football coach might define success as winning a national championship. A college student might define success as earning a degree . . . a salesman, as being number one in the company . . . a parent, as raising godly children.

Definitions come and go, depending on whom you ask and when you ask. Generally speaking, many people define success as "setting a goal and accomplishing it." That definition, however, is very limited. A person might set an evil goal or a good goal. The *nature* of the goals that we set is a key factor in success, and especially so if we are dealing with God's view of success.

As Christians, our goals must not be defined in terms of "my will;" our goals must be rooted in what we know to be "God's will." Our human approach tends to say, "Here's what I want to do and what I want to accomplish." A Christian's approach must be, "Here is what I believe God wants me to be and to do, and here's how I can become that type of person and accomplish those tasks." The Christian faces the challenge of *being* a godly person, then *obeying* God's Word. Our lives as Christians are not to be wrapped up in what we earn or own. Life for the Christian is wrapped up in who we *are* in Christ Jesus.

This study guide is based upon the following definition of success:

> Success is desiring to be the person that God has called me to be and to achieve those goals that God has helped me to set.

An ungodly person cannot be genuinely successful according to this definition. An ungodly person might amass a certain degree of material wealth, achieve a certain degree of fame, gain a certain number of degrees or awards, attain a certain level of social privilege, or acquire a certain degree of political power, but the ungodly person cannot be truly successful in his life because he does not desire to be the *person* that God has called him to be. He is achieving *his* goals, not God's goals. He is defining his life according to his own lusts, desires, and purposes rather than seeking to line up his life with God's purposes.

The world tends to sum up success as fame and fortune. God sums up success in terms of relationship, character, and obedience. He wants us to succeed first and foremost in our relationship with Him, then in our relationships with others, and then in our vocations and ministries. The godly person who is pursuing God's plan and purposes for his life may experience wealth, prominence, and status as side benefits, but these are not to be the Christian's primary goals and objectives.

The True Rewards of God-Based Success

The true rewards associated with God's success are the intangibles that all people want. The self-focused person may think he desires fame and fortune, but in the end every person desires inner peace, joy, contentment, health and wholeness (spirit, mind, and body), feelings of spiritual security, the hope of eternal life, family love, and a living relationship with God. On more than one occasion, I have heard a wealthy or famous person say, "I'd trade it all for a little tranquility and a secure hope that I know what is going to happen to me after I die." I have heard so-called successful people say, "I'd trade everything I have for an hour of pure love, an hour without pain, or an hour of knowing that I have done what God created me to do."

Those who limit their pursuit in life only to fame and fortune wind up frustrated, disappointed, and with a gaping void in their lives that they cannot fill. Those who choose first to pursue the life for which God designed them and to which God calls them experience the real "richness" of life and the hope of everlasting life.

The Most Important Question You Can Ask

The most important question you can ask about your success is, "What does the Lord want me to be and to do today?" That is a question to ask every day. Success, according to our definition above, is an *ongoing pursuit*. It is establishing and accomplishing God-given goals that the Lord sets for our lives. It is refusing to become discouraged, disheartened, or dissuaded from God's goals. It is a *continuing* desire to be the person that God calls us to be and to achieve the goals that God helps us to set.

No person can ever reach the horizon, and in the same way no person can ever truly achieve success. Success is not a quantity that can be measured or a concept that can be fully defined. Success is a concept embedded in a *process*. Our understanding of success grows as we mature in Christ. It is something that continually lies ahead of us and continually develops within us.

The Holy Spirit works in us in a unique way. He allows us to experience great joy and satisfaction in the present moment of our lives, and at the same time He calls us to yet greater conformity to Christ Jesus, to greater desires for ministry, and to greater tasks in establishing God's purposes on the earth.

The Christian always has a hunger in his heart to be more like Christ, to draw nearer to the heart of God, and to know more about the truth that

God presents in His Word. A Christian always has a thirst to experience more of the goodness of God, to serve Him with greater consistency and effectiveness, and to bear more and more eternal fruit. The quest to satisfy that hunger and thirst is the quest of success. It is a lifelong quest. It is also the most satisfying way a person might ever live.

What Is Your Desire Today?

Genuine success from God's point of view is rooted in what God sets as the goals for our lives. It is rooted in the relationship that God desires to have with us. It begins within us the moment we say to the Lord, "It's not what I want to be that matters—it's who You want me to be. It's not what I want to do that counts—it's what You want me to do that is my goal."

What are your desires today regarding your own success? What are your answers to these three key questions:

1. Do you truly desire to be a success from God's point of view?

2. Do you desire to be all that God calls you to be in Christ Jesus?

3. Do you desire to do all that the Lord directs you to do on a day-to-day basis?

⛭ What is your own definition of success? How does that definition compare with God's definition?

∾ In what areas do you feel that you have experienced success in life so far? In what areas do you feel that you have not succeeded as yet?

Beloved, I pray that you may prosper in all things and be in health, just as your soul prospers. For I rejoiced greatly when brethren came and testified of the truth that is in you, just as you walk in the truth. I have no greater joy than to hear that my children walk in truth.

—3 John 2–4

∾ How would you define a "prosperous soul"? What constitutes prosperity for a person's soul? What constitutes failure?

What does it mean to "walk in the truth"? How is this done? How does it affect a person's success in life?

Today and Tomorrow

Today: God defines success as doing things His way rather than my own way.

Tomorrow: I will adopt God's definition of success rather than the world's.

LESSON 2

God's Commitment to Your Success

─────── ❧ **In This Lesson** ❧ ───────

LEARNING: DOES GOD REALLY CARE WHETHER OR NOT I'M SUCCESSFUL?

GROWING: WHAT ROLE DOES HE PLAY, AND WHAT ROLE DO I PLAY IN THE PROCESS?

God desires your success, and He is committed to helping His people become successful. He wants His people to be blessed and to experience whole-person prosperity. Nehemiah believed and claimed God's success for himself. He heard news that the walls and gates of Jerusalem lay in ruins, so he began to fast and pray about the situation. The king noticed his sorrow and authorized Nehemiah to go to Jerusalem and make repairs to the city.

When Nehemiah arrived in Jerusalem, he immediately faced opposition from those who did not want him to succeed in the task before him. He responded to those who opposed him by saying:

> The God of heaven Himself will prosper us; therefore we His servants will arise and build, but you have no heritage or right or memorial in Jerusalem.

> —Nehemiah 2:20

☙ What did Nehemiah expect God to do for him, according to this verse? In what ways did Nehemiah expect to prosper?

☙ What did Nehemiah have to do himself, according to this verse? What part does personal responsibility play in achieving success?

Four Aspects of God's Commitment to Success

The Bible presents four basic concepts that are important for you to grasp if you are to understand God's commitment to your success.

1. God wants you to live successfully regardless of your outer circumstances. Perhaps no person in the Bible experienced more difficult circumstances in his life than Daniel. Daniel was taken captive by the Babylonians when he was a young man. He was forced to live in an alien culture the rest of his life and to serve three heathen kings. On several occasions, he had to stand in opposition to the king's magicians. On one occasion, his opposition resulted in facing a den of lions. Yet we read in Daniel 6:28, "So this Daniel prospered in the reign of Darius and in the reign of Cyrus the Persian." Daniel lived well and lived successfully in the midst of his circumstances. We are called to do the same.

Too often we look at our outward circumstances and conclude, "God must not want to prosper me." We must never look to outward circumstances, including our past failures, and use them as a reason to doubt God's desire to prosper us. True prosperity begins in the heart and soul of a person. True prosperity is always a possibility for us, because change and spiritual growth are always possible for the Christian.

2. Your success is directly related to your faith. To be successful, a person must first believe that he can be successful. The real question for the Christian is, "Believe in what? Have faith in whom?" When we identify the object of our faith, we know the foundation for our success. If you are putting your faith in God to help you become a success, then your foundation is as strong as He is!

But without faith it is impossible to please Him, for he who comes to God must believe that He is, and that He is a rewarder of those who diligently seek Him.

—Hebrews 11:6

⤙ Why is it impossible to please God without faith? What role does faith play in achieving success?

⤙ Why must we believe that God exists before we can come before Him? Why must we also believe that He is "a rewarder"?

3. *God's commitment to our success is related to our courage and to our obedience in keeping His commandments.* As Joshua prepared to lead the Israelites across the Jordan River to claim the Promised Land, God spoke these words to him:

> Be strong and very courageous, that you may observe to do according to all the law which Moses My servant commanded you; do not turn from it to the right hand or to the left, that you may prosper wherever you go. This Book of the Law shall not depart from your mouth, but you shall meditate in it day and night, that you may observe to do according to all that is

written in it. For then you will make your way prosperous, and then you will have good success. Have I not commanded you? Be strong and of good courage; do not be afraid, nor be dismayed, for the Lord your God is with you wherever you go.

—Joshua 1:7–9

The issue for Christians is not whether God is committed to their success, but whether we are committed to keeping God's commandments, having courage, using our faith, and choosing to believe for success regardless of the outer circumstances of our lives.

∽ What role does courage play in being successful?

∽ Why did God tell Joshua that he needed courage to obey His laws? Why is such obedience necessary for success?

4. The Bible presents success as a process, not a destination. Living successfully does not mean that you are going to live on a mountaintop with a big grin on your face and a blue ribbon attached to your lapel every day of your life. High points may come at times—and they may be virtually nonexistent at other times. Success is to be found in the way in which we live out our lives day in and day out. It is to be found as we pursue what God calls us to do. Success is not the end of a process; it is *the way that we undertake the process called life.*

God Wants You to Succeed

God gives us abundant evidence in His Word that He wants us to be successful. We see that evidence in at least four areas:

1. Each of us has a built-in desire for success. Every baby comes into this world goal-oriented. He has a built-in desire to get his needs met and to take control of his world. He has a desire to learn to communicate and to become mobile—to scoot, to crawl, to walk. God has built a desire for success into us so that we will act. This drive can motivate us toward the things of God or the things of our own flesh: "the lust of the flesh, the lust of the eyes, and the pride of life" (1 John 2:16). It is up to us how we will choose to act on the built-in desire toward success, satisfaction, and fulfillment.

Do not let your heart envy sinners, but be zealous for the fear of the Lord all the day; for surely there is a hereafter, and your hope will not be cut off. Hear, my son, and be wise; and guide your heart in the way.

—Proverbs 23:17–19

What does it mean to "be zealous for the fear of the Lord"? What is the "fear of the Lord"? How does this influence success?

What role does envy play in our success or failure? Why is it so dangerous for a Christian?

2. God has equipped you for success. God has given you natural talents and abilities, as well as one or more spiritual gifts. These gifts have been grafted into your unique personality for one reason: so that you might use them to produce quality work that has a potential for both earthly and eternal reward. It is up to each of us to discover our gifts and then to develop them to the best of our ability. That takes practice and discipline—both of which God provides to us when we ask.

> Every good gift and every perfect gift is from above, and comes down from the Father of lights, with whom there is no variation or shadow of turning.
>
> —James 1:17

⤸ What does James mean that there is "no variation or shadow of turning" in God's character? What does this have to do with His gifts?

⤸ How do the world's gifts differ from God's gifts? How does the world's idea of success differ from God's version of success?

3. The Lord has given us His Holy Spirit to help us succeed. The Holy Spirit has been given to every believer to

    ❦ perfect our gifts.
    ❦ give strength to us in our areas of weakness.
    ❦ give us daily guidance into the ways in which we should go, including decisions and opportunities.

The Holy Spirit works within us to renew our strength, sharpen our senses, and help us get the most work done in the most efficient manner. It is the Holy Spirit who uses our gifts in helping or blessing others. The Holy Spirit also directs us toward those who need what we have been equipped to give .When we yield ourselves and our gifts to the Holy Spirit, He comforts us and reassures us that all things *are* working together for our good from God's perspective (Rom. 8:28). The Holy Spirit is God's gift to us to *enable* our success.

> However, when He, the Spirit of truth, has come, He will guide you into all truth; for He will not speak on His own authority, but whatever He hears He will speak; and He will tell you things to come.

> —John 16:13

∾ What is the source of the Holy Spirit's guidance, according to this verse? How does this source of truth guarantee your success?

∾ If the Holy Spirit is capable of telling us of things to come, what effect will this have on your success today?

Never dismiss or diminish the value of what the Lord has given you for your success. We must refuse to discount the gifts that we have been given, which is what we do when we say things such as:

- "I don't have enough formal education."
- "I was born at the wrong time on the wrong side of the tracks."
- "I'm too old."
- "I've got circumstances that will forever keep me from being successful."

God has uniquely gifted you to be a success in a unique calling that He has for your life. No excuse is justified in His presence. In whatever area you may feel weak or inadequate, His presence and power are more than sufficient!

4. God has given you the power of prayer so that you might use it to further your success. Every one of us has the privilege of bowing before God every morning of our lives and saying, "Lord, I need Your help. I need Your guidance. I need Your strength and wisdom." The Lord delights in our prayers that request His help. He delights in our expressions of faith in Him to help us succeed at what He calls us to do. Prayer is a powerful tool that God wants you to use in becoming *all* that He wants you to be.

> You lust and do not have. You murder and covet and cannot obtain. You fight and war. Yet you do not have because you do not ask. You ask and do not receive, because you ask amiss, that you may spend it on your pleasures.
>
> —James 4:2, 3

⚞ What do lust, murder, coveting, fighting, and war have to do with the world's ideas of success? How do they compare with God's definition of success?

.

⚞ According to James, what two things are necessary if we are to receive success from God?

What wonderful gifts God has given to us! He has given each person a desire to succeed—in other words, He has given us the motivation that we need to pursue success. He has give us talents and abilities; when we develop them and use them for His purposes, we can be assured of success. He has given us the Holy Spirit to strengthen us in our areas of weakness and to give us daily counsel into the right choices to become successful. And He has given us the privilege of prayer so that we might activate our faith and use it to bring about the character and courage He wants us to have. God wants us to know how to be successful, and He has given us all that we need to be successful in reality.

↪ Today and Tomorrow ↩

TODAY: GOD IS DEEPLY COMMITTED TO MY SUCCESS—ACCORDING TO HIS DEFINITION.

TOMORROW: I WILL SPEND TIME THIS WEEK IN PRAYER, ASKING THE LORD TO GUIDE ME EACH DAY.

LESSON 3

Setting Godly Goals

────── ❧ **In This Lesson** ❧ ──────

LEARNING: WHAT ARE GODLY GOALS?

GROWING: HOW CAN I ACHIEVE THE GOALS THAT I SET?

────────── ⊰⊱ ──────────

One of the most important questions you can ever ask is, "What goals does *God* want me to set to be a success in His eyes?" Setting *God's* goals for your life is a critical step toward being a success in God's eyes. One of the most goal-oriented people in the Bible is the apostle Paul. In writing to the Philippians, Paul said,

> But what things were gain to me, these I have counted loss for Christ. Yet indeed I also count all things loss for the excellence of the knowledge of Christ Jesus my Lord, for whom I have suffered the loss of all things, and count them as rubbish, that they may gain Christ and be found in Him . . . that I may know Him and the power of His resurrection, and the fellowship of His sufferings, being conformed to His death, if, by any means, I may attain to the resurrection from the dead. Not that I have already attained, or am already perfected; but I press on, that I may lay hold of that for which Christ Jesus has also laid hold of me. Brethren, I do not count myself to have apprehended; but one thing I do, forgetting those things which are behind and reaching forward to those things which are ahead, I press

toward the goal for the prize of the upward call of God in Christ Jesus.

—Philippians 3:7–14

∼ What things have you gained in life? When have you worked hard to gain something, only to realize later that it was not as worthwhile as you had expected?

∼ What does it mean to know the power of Jesus' resurrection? What does it mean to know the fellowship of His sufferings? When have you experienced either of these?

Paul was not a man who wasted time or energy. He was extremely focused in his life, and he had an overwhelming sense of purpose and direction. He clearly stated his life goals to the Philippians:

∼ to know Christ Jesus as intimately as possible
∼ to experience the righteousness of Christ in his own life
∼ to be conformed to Christ in every way

We know from the description of Paul's ministry in Acts that he also had another goal: to reach as many people as possible with the message of Jesus Christ's crucifixion and resurrection, and to do so with a sense of urgency. Paul made no claim that he had achieved his life goals. Rather, he stated that he was continuing to *press* toward the goal of the prize of the "upward call of God in Christ Jesus." To *press*, in this case, means "to diligently follow after." Paul was zealous in following Christ.

> I have been crucified with Christ; it is no longer I who live, but Christ lives in me; and the life which I now live in the flesh I live by faith in the Son of God, who loved me and gave Himself for me.

> —Galatians 2:20

What does it mean to be "crucified with Christ"? How is this done in practical terms?

What role does this process play in achieving God's definition of success?

What Are Godly Goals?

A goal is an aim, a purpose, a sense of direction toward which a person moves all of his energies, desires, and efforts. Goals are the "targets" toward which we point our lives. A goal involves an organized, planned "stretching" of your life. If you have already achieved something, it is no longer a goal—it is an accomplishment. A goal is a statement of how you desire to grow, develop, or mature in a specific and achievable way.

Goals for the Christian are not based upon how we desire to live for our own pleasure and satisfaction. Rather, we live as unto the Lord. We are *His* possession, bought with a price—the precious blood of Jesus Christ. We belong to God, and our goals must be ones that bring pleasure to Him.

> I beseech you therefore, brethren, by the mercies of God, that you present your bodies a living sacrifice, holy, acceptable to God, which is your reasonable service. And do not be conformed to this world, but be transformed by the renewing of your mind, that you may prove what is that good and acceptable and perfect will of God.
>
> —Romans 12:1, 2

∾ What does it mean to present your bodies as a living sacrifice? Give some real life examples.

☙ How does a person become conformed to this world? What results when that happens?

☙ How does a person renew his mind? What role does this play in achieving God's definition of success?

I have found it very helpful in my life to identify and to write down my priority goal: "To know Christ as intimately and fully as possible." My secondary goal sets the pattern for my life and determines the details of my daily schedule: "To get the gospel of Jesus Christ to as many people as possible, as clearly as possible, by the power of the Holy Spirit and to the glory of God." That's why I live. I encourage you to reflect upon your priority goal in life, and to state your priority goal and your secondary goals in writing.

☙ What is your priority goal? Give practical examples of how this goal will shape your life in the coming week.

⁊ What are your secondary goals? Give practical examples of how these goals will shape your life in the coming week.

Goals help a person maintain focus. They help a person avoid stray relationships and activities that can become distractions and deterrents. They help a person set his schedule over long periods of time, as well as daily. Goals help put life in balance. Take a look at the chart below and consider your own life:

Person with No Goals	Person with Goals
Adrift	Sense of direction
No excitement in living	Excitement in living
Accepts mediocrity	Pursues excellence
Critical of those who succeed	Appreciates those who succeed
Disappointed with life	Strong sense of purpose and value
Content to live in a rut	Seeks a creative, active life
Bad steward of time, energy, resources	Seeks a balanced life of emotional and physical health

⁊ Which column best describes your own life? Which areas need work to become a more goal-oriented Christian?

Should Christians Set Goals for the Future?

There are those in the body of Christ who contend that Christians should not set goals. I want to take a look at two main passages of Scripture that critics of goal-setting often use to support their belief.

The Case for Contentment

The first passage often used to teach that goal-setting is not biblical is Hebrews 13:5:

> Let your conduct be without covetousness; be content with such things as you have. For He Himself has said, "I will never leave you nor forsake you."

Contentment in the context of this verse is in direct relationship to the statement, "Let your conduct be without covetousness." We are never to covet what others have. Contentment is realizing that God is the Source of all that we need for our present happiness. It is being thankful for what the Lord is providing, even as we plan for our future. It is trusting that the Lord will never leave us nor forsake us. It is experiencing the peace of God in the midst of any circumstance or situation, even as we make our requests known to God.

Contentment is not settling for a mediocre life. Rather, it is a feeling of being at rest in our relationship with the Lord, even as we pursue greater wholeness and prosperity.

How is contentment the opposite of coveting? What causes coveting? How can it be avoided?

⌘ What is the key to contentment, according to Hebrews 13:5? In practical terms, how does a person find contentment?

Living Each Day as It Comes

Matthew 6:31–34 is often used to counteract a need for goal-setting:

> "Therefore do not worry, saying, 'What shall we eat?' or 'What shall we drink?' or 'What shall we wear?' For after all these things the Gentiles seek. For your heavenly Father knows that you need all these things. But seek first the kingdom of God and His righteousness, and all these things shall be added to you. Therefore do not worry about tomorrow, for tomorrow will worry about its own things. Sufficient for the day is its own trouble."

This passage has nothing to do with planning or not planning. Rather, it is about feeling anxious about whether God will provide our day-to-day needs for food, shelter, and clothing. It also provides a great statement about our priorities. Jesus says that we are to seek *first* the kingdom of God and His righteousness. Seeking the kingdom of God and His righteousness is a *goal*. It is the foremost thing worth pursuing and worth establishing in one's life.

Seeking the kingdom of God and His righteousness does not happen automatically. It happens because we set our minds and hearts toward those things that build our inner character and yield eternal reward.

31

⤙ In practical terms, what does it mean to seek God's kingdom? To seek His righteousness? Why do we need to actively seek these things?

⤙ What role does worry play in a person's view of success or failure? Why does Jesus command us not to worry?

Four Questions to Ask About the Goals You Set

As you set any goal in your life, ask yourself these four questions:

1. Why, Lord, is this important to You? If you understand the answer to why a goal is important to the Lord, you'll be in a good position to seek answers to other questions: How? When? Where? With whom?

2. Lord, does this fit into Your plan for my life? Some tasks may be good, but not be God's best for you. Ask the Lord what fits you best, given your talents, abilities, and skills.

3. Is this goal totally in line with God's Word? God will not lead you to pursue a goal that is contrary to the principles established in the Bible.

4. How might the accomplishment of this goal bring blessing to others? God gives us goals so that He might do two things simultaneously: perform a refining work in our lives, and perform a work that will benefit others and be for their eternal good.

🕭 Which of your goals do not meet these four criteria? Which ones do?

> If then you were raised with Christ, seek those things which are above, where Christ is, sitting at the right hand of God. Set your mind on things above, not on things on the earth.
>
> —Colossians 3:1, 2

🕭 What sort of goals pursue "things on the earth"? Give practical examples.

What sort of goals pursue "things above"? How are these different from earthly goals?

Writing Down Your Goals

It is important that you write down your goals. The Lord said to Jeremiah, "Write in a book for yourself all the words that I have spoken to you" (Jer. 30:2; see also Jer. 36:2). The Lord said to the prophet Habakkuk,

> Write the vision
> And make it plain on tablets,
> That he may run who reads it.
>
> —Habakkuk 2:2

Put a Date with a Goal

Some goals are lifelong, but even lifelong goals can be broken down into smaller goals that can be accomplished in short- and medium-range periods. Identify your goals that are

❧ immediate: things to be done each day, or to be accomplished in a week or month;

❧ short-range: those goals that may take one to three months or even as long as a year;

❧ long-range: those goals that may extend beyond a year.

Consider All Areas of Your Life

Goals can be set in each of life's main areas:

❧ Spiritual
❧ Personal
❧ Family
❧ Vocation
❧ Social
❧ Financial

Take a look at the goals that you believe are God's plan for you. Do you have goals in each of these areas? Do your goals tend to cluster mainly in one or two areas? If you are neglecting certain areas of your life, or are placing too much emphasis on one or two areas, your life is not truly balanced. Seek to establish wholeness.

Be Specific

State precisely what you intend to accomplish—avoid fuzzy generalities. Jesus met Bartimaeus at the outskirts of Jericho and asked him one simple question: "What do you want Me to do for you?" (Mark 10:51). Jesus could see that Bartimaeus was blind, yet He asked him this question so that he might confront his need and face the prospect of his own healing. Do you truly desire the specifics of the goals that you have written down? Why do you want to accomplish what you have stated as goals? What are your motives? Do you truly want to live the way you would live if your goals were accomplished?

Set Goals that You Cannot Reach on Your Own Strength

A truly God-given goal always has a faith factor to it. It is a goal that will stretch you, challenge you, cause you to grow in spirit, and cause you to rely on God for help, wisdom, strength, and results.

Take one step at a time as you establish your goals. Wait upon the Lord for His direction and guidance. Test your goals against the Scriptures and see if they endure over time. Few things worth attaining can be accomplished in a day. What matters most is our slow, steadfast, obedient pursuit of those goals to which God calls us. He is as concerned about our ongoing faithfulness, discipline, obedience, and reliance upon Him as He is about our accomplishing the goals that He helps us establish.

> I have been crucified with Christ; it is no longer I who live, but Christ lives in me; and the life which I now live in the flesh I live by faith in the Son of God, who loved me and gave Himself for me.
>
> —Galatians 2:20

☙ If you have been crucified in Christ, what effect does that have on your personal success or failure? What role does Christ play, according to this verse?

What role does faith play in your success, according to this verse? How can faith lead to success? How can a lack of faith lead to failure?

Today and Tomorrow

TODAY: GOD WANTS ME TO SET GOALS FOR THE FUTURE, AND HE IS READY TO HELP ME DEFINE THEM TODAY.

TOMORROW: I WILL SPEND TIME THIS WEEK PRAYERFULLY CREATING A LIST OF GOALS FOR MY LIFE.

Lesson 4

God's Personal Success Patterns for You

──────── ❧ **In This Lesson** ❧ ────────

LEARNING: HOW DOES GOD'S PLAN FOR SUCCESS APPLY TO MY UNIQUE CIRCUMSTANCES?

GROWING: WHAT ROLE DO I PLAY IN THIS PROCESS?

──────── ∽∞∾ ────────

One of the greatest differences between the world's message about success and God's plan for success is that the world seeks one formula that produces one set of results for all people. God's plan is far more creative, far more individualized, and far more personal. His *principles* don't change, but God's formula for success always takes into account your unique set of spiritual gifts, natural talents, personality, and circumstances. In this lesson, we are going to take a look at the lives of three men who portrayed distinctly different patterns of success.

God's Pattern of Success for Joseph

Joseph had an understanding of God's personal success plan for his life even when he was young. He was given divine insight into God's plan for his future, which included great prominence, power, and prestige. His understanding of his personal future success was based upon two dreams that God gave him when he was only seventeen years old. (You can read about these dreams in Genesis 37:5–9.)

Like many people today, Joseph had a dream of success, but no *plan* for success. God had given him a glimpse of his future but had not provided the intervening details. It was up to Joseph to pursue God's plan for success with faith and obedience by doing the things that the Lord put in his path to do.

> Show me Your ways, O Lord; teach me Your paths. Lead me in Your truth and teach me, for You are the God of my salvation; on You I wait all the day.
>
> —Psalm 25:4, 5

What is God's role in teaching you about His definition of success? What is your role in that process?

Joseph's dreams were prophecies of the future given to him by God. How does God use His Word to lead us to success? How does He use our personal desires?

God never asks any of us to sit down and wait idly for Him to vault us into success. He asks us to trust and obey Him day by day, and to learn the lessons that He sets before us. Some of the work that God gives us may seem menial and totally unrelated to the end result of our success. What we often do not perceive is that God is building into us a strong pattern of experience, skill, trustworthiness, honesty, integrity, and character, so that we will be ready when the time comes for us to be in a position of authority or influence.

The success that we achieve is never of our own doing. God's hand is always in both the process and the results. Joseph knew this. He persevered with faith in God through abandonment by his brothers, slavery in a foreign land, false accusations, and imprisonment, and through those experiences he was prepared to exercise authority with wisdom. Joseph made wise decisions, and he gave God the glory for bringing him to a position in which he could help his family and countless others. He said to his brothers later in his life,

> God sent me before you to preserve a posterity for you in the earth, and to save your lives by a great deliverance. So now it was not you who sent me here, but God; and He has made me a father to Pharaoh, and lord of all his house, and a ruler throughout all the land of Egypt.
>
> —Genesis 45:7, 8

Joseph's brothers had sold him into slavery. How, then, could he truthfully say that it was not his brothers who had sent him to Egypt?

How does God use the mundane events of your life to prepare you for His future plans for you? What part do you play in that process?

The success plan for Joseph's life might be summarized like this:

❦ *Vision* ❦

followed by years of

❦ *faithful preparation, trust, and obedience* ❦

resulting in years of

❦ *service, authority, and reward* ❦

And we know that all things work together for good to those who love God, to those who are the called according to His purpose.

—Romans 8:28

❧ How does this verse apply to the story of Joseph? How does it apply in your own life?

❧ What is the difference between all things *being* good and all things *working together for* good? How is this difference illustrated in Joseph's life? In your life?

God's Pattern of Success for Moses

The pattern for success that we see in Moses's life is very different from that of Joseph. Moses did not have a vision for success early in his life, although he experienced a certain degree of privilege as an adopted son of Pharaoh. He grew up separated from his people. After murdering an Egyptian, he ran for his life to the remote desert region of Midian, and there he married and spent nearly forty years tending sheep. Then the day came when the Lord revealed Himself to Moses and gave him a specific mission for his life.

Moses argued with god about his worthiness to pursue the goals that God set before him. He eventually relented and went to Pharaoh with the message from God, "Let My people go." For forty years, Moses led the Israelites out of Egypt, across the wilderness, to the Promised Land. The success pattern that the Lord had for him was this:

Seemingly unrelated events

without the person having a vision of success, followed by a

definite and specific call of God

followed by

faithful obedience and trust

A similar pattern might be seen in the life of the apostle Paul. Paul grew up studying God's Law and being the best Pharisee and Roman citizen he could possibly be. Then came his experience on the Damascus Road in which he surrendered his life to Christ. Suddenly, Paul's life began to make sense. He could see ways in which he had been perfectly prepared for the plan that God had for him. He knew the Scriptures, so he could explain with depth and clarity how Christ Jesus fulfilled them. He had the freedom to travel and speak freely throughout the Roman empire. He knew the Jews and their customs and had access to their synagogues. He also knew that God could redeem even the hardened sinful heart, and he was quick to extend the mercy of God to the Gentiles.

Can you see ways in which the Lord has built into you the abilities, skills, and readiness to take on the challenges that He is now presenting to you?

For I know the thoughts that I think toward you, says the LORD, thoughts of peace and not of evil, to give you a future and a hope. Then you will call upon Me and go and pray to Me, and I will listen to you. And you will seek Me and find Me, when you search for Me with all your heart.

—Jeremiah 29:11–13

How might Moses or Joseph have felt that life was hopeless, that the future was bleak, at times in their lives? When have you felt that way?

↪ How did God ultimately demonstrate that He had been preparing those men for His great plans? How can their examples encourage you to trust in God's faithfulness?

God's Pattern of Success for David

There is a third pattern of success that we see in the life of King David. He came to a knowledge of the Lord as a youngster, was anointed by God for a great future as a teenager, and experienced a series of visible and outward successes throughout his life, one building upon another.

This does not mean that David did not encounter difficult times. These situations, however, strengthened David and further prepared him for greater things ahead. How was it that David was not defeated by jealousy, exile, warring enemies, traitorous followers, rebellious children, or even his own sinfulness? He was not defeated because, in each instance, David turned to the Lord in repentance and in trust. Any detours or mistakes were quickly reversed through David's repentant heart, his humility before the Lord, and his desire to serve God fully. David never stopped acknowledging God as the Source of his strength.

The pattern of David's success might be described this way:

⤳ Anointing by God ⤳

followed by

⤳ success built upon success ⤳

The apostle Peter seems to have experienced a similar pattern for success in his life. Peter was a successful fisherman when Jesus first met him, and he continued to enjoy a great deal of success as he followed Jesus. He was one of Jesus' inner circle, along with James and John, and he was the apostle to whom Jesus spoke the most.

Peter certainly had failures and made mistakes. He rebuked Jesus when Jesus spoke of His crucifixion; he failed in his faith when it came to calming a storm; he relied on his own strength when he cut off the ear of a high priest's servant; and he denied Jesus three times after Jesus' arrest. But these were all incidents of which Peter quickly repented.

After the resurrection of Jesus, it was Peter who became the leader of the church. It was Peter who preached a sermon on the day of Pentecost that resulted in three thousand members being added to the newly established church. It was Peter who brought healing to the lame man at the Beautiful Gate, who raised a paralyzed man from his bed, and who raised Dorcas from the dead—all in the name of Jesus. It was Peter who opened the door to the Gentiles, who defended the rights of the Gentile Christians, and who established the earliest believers in the teachings of Jesus.

Many Christians today are raised in godly homes, and they come to know the Lord early in their lives. Then the Lord seems to direct them into a very specific avenue of ministry or service. They continue to grow and mature, becoming increasingly conformed to Christ. Their effectiveness as witnesses to Christ also continues to grow. Their life pattern is one of moving from strength to strength.

For whom He foreknew, He also predestined to be conformed
to the image of His Son, that He might be the firstborn among
many brethren. Moreover whom He predestined, these He also
called; whom He called, these He also justified; and whom He
justified, these He also glorified.

—Romans 8:29, 30

⤸ What does it mean to "be conformed to the image" of Jesus?
How is this accomplished, in practical terms?

⤸ According to these verses, what role does God play in this
process? What role do you play?

A Unique Pattern for Each Person

Was Joseph more successful than Moses? Was King David more successful than Joseph? No! Each was successful in his own life *according
to the pattern that God had established for him.* God does not deal
with any one of us exactly as He deals with another person. Even if God
seems to be implementing one of the three patterns described in this
lesson, the exact circumstances that He allows in our lives are unique,
and His call to each of us is also unique.

Never covet another person's success. Never discount what the Lord is doing in your life. To do so is to greatly hinder the work that God desires to do in you, and you may stall the fulfillment of God's success plan for your life.

> But you, O man of God, flee these things and pursue righteousness, godliness, faith, love, patience, gentleness. Fight the good fight of faith, lay hold on eternal life, to which you were also called and have confessed the good confession in the presence of many witnesses.
>
> —1 Timothy 6:11, 12

🕭 Define the following in your own words, and give practical examples of each:

Righteousness:

Godliness:

Faith:

Love:

Patience:

Gentleness:

What role does fighting have in each of the above? In what sense must a Christian "lay hold" of such things?

Today and Tomorrow

TODAY: GOD HAS A UNIQUE PLAN FOR ME, BUT IT INCLUDES TOTAL SUCCESS AND NOT FAILURE.

TOMORROW: I WILL STUDY THE LIVES OF BIBLICAL SAINTS THIS WEEK, ASKING THE LORD TO SHOW ME HOW THEY CAN BE EXAMPLES FOR ME TO FOLLOW.

Lesson 5

Pursuing God's Goals

── ❧ In This Lesson ❧ ──

LEARNING: Once I've established God's goals, how do I attain them?

GROWING: How can I overcome my fears of failure?

If I were to draw a line in front of you today and say, "Step over this line, and your life will be better, beginning today," would you step over that line? I feel certain that you would! I give you that challenge today regarding the pursuit of your own goals, because it is not enough for a person to set goals or to recognize the ways in which God is working in his life. We each must make a decision to *pursue* God's goals and to pursue them God's way.

Doing Things God's Way

The way that we reach our goals is critical to our being successful in attaining the goals that God helps us set, and also in developing the character that God wants us to have. The principles for *how* to reach our God-given goals can be found in the story of David and Goliath.

The army of the Philistines was encamped on one side of a valley, and the army of Israel was on the other side. For forty consecutive days, the champion of the Philistines—Goliath, their number-one warrior—had come out and stood in front of his army and shouted to the Israelites, "I defy the armies of Israel this day; give me a man, that we may fight together" (1 Sam. 17:10). Goliath and the Philistines set the terms for the battle. They wanted the contest to be one man versus one man; if the Philistines won, all the Israelites would become their servants. A great deal was at stake, and day after day the Israelites failed to respond to Goliath's challenge.

Many of us find ourselves in the same position when it comes to the pursuit of our goals. We see a giant obstacle standing between where we are at present and where we want to be. That obstacle fills us with fear; it holds out the prospect of defeat and loss. We fail to act.

☙ When has fear prevented you from pursuing a godly goal? How might you do things if you could turn back the clock?

Ten Aspects of Pursuing a Goal God's Way

David arrived on the scene and was angered by what he heard and saw. He immediately established a goal that he believed was what God wanted him to accomplish. There are ten important aspects of David's goal setting.

1. A Clear Picture of the Goal and Its Rewards

Upon hearing Goliath's challenge, David asked, "What shall be done for the man who kills this Philistine and takes away the reproach from Israel? For who is this uncircumcised Philistine, that he should defy the armies of the living God?" (1 Sam. 17:26). David's questions were firmly rooted in his belief that Goliath needed to be defeated, could be defeated, and *would* be defeated. He saw the killing of Goliath as an achievable goal and certainly one that must have rewards associated with it.

At this time, David had already been anointed to be the next king of Israel, although only he and the prophet Samuel knew about it. For David, the victory over Goliath was not a personal act of bravery as much as an act of a future king on behalf of his people. David fully expected to be successful in his pursuit of God's goals for his life, and he expected to rule a people who were free of the Philistines, not slaves to them.

Notice David's concern: to take away the reproach from Israel. What does this reveal about his goals? What might another man have sought by fighting Goliath?

How did David perceive Goliath's impudent challenge? Who was actually being mocked by the Philistines? What does this reveal about David's priorities?

2. A Consuming Desire to Reach the Goal

David could not be talked out of pursuing his goal. His brothers tried to dissuade him, but he refused to leave, refused to be discouraged, and refused to quit talking about Goliath's defeat. If your goals are from the Lord, you will have a feeling deep within you that you *must* accomplish them in order to be obedient to the Lord and to bring benefit to others.

> But it is good to be zealous in a good thing always, and not only when I am present with you.

> —Galatians 4:18

When have you been zealous in doing something good? What fueled your zeal?

When have you faced strong opposition while trying to obey the Lord's commands? Where did that opposition originate?

3. Confidence in the Lord's Help

David had no doubt that, with the Lord's help, he would be able to kill Goliath. He boldly said to King Saul, "Let no man's heart fail because of him; your servant will go and fight with the Philistine" (1 Sam. 17:32). David wasn't confident in his own ability. He boldly stated, "The Lord . . . will deliver me from the hand of this Philistine" (v. 37). He then rushed down the mountainside toward Goliath crying, "This day the Lord will deliver you into my hand . . . that all the earth may know that there is a God in Israel. Then all this assembly shall know that the Lord does not save with sword and spear; for the battle is the Lord's, and He will give you into our hands" (1 Sam. 17:46, 47).

So we may boldly say: "The Lord is my helper; I will not fear. What can man do to me?"

—Hebrews 13:6

⚞ What made David so confident that God would give him victory against Goliath? What did he expect God to do? What did God expect him to do?

⚞ How did David's response to the Philistines differ from the that of Israel's army? How did David know that this was a time for action, rather than inaction?

4. A Course for Action

David didn't go into battle without first getting Saul's approval. He went through the right channels (see 1 Sam. 17:37). David then chose the right armor and the right method for the upcoming battle. He went into battle with weapons that were right for his unique experience and skills. Too often we try to accomplish our goals using man-made methods that may work for another person, but which are totally unsuited to our abilities and talents. Trust God to reveal to you *His* method for pursuing *your* success.

> So Saul clothed David with his armor, and he put a bronze helmet on his head; he also clothed him with a coat of mail. David fastened his sword to his armor and tried to walk, for he had not tested them. And David said to Saul, "I cannot walk with these, for I have not tested them." So David took them off. Then he took his staff in his hand; and he chose for himself five smooth stones from the brook, and put them in a shepherd's bag, in a pouch which he had, and his sling was in his hand. And he drew near to the Philistine.
>
> —1 Samuel 17:38–40

Why did David reject Saul's armor? Why did he choose a staff and sling instead?

What unique skills and gifts has God given you? How can you use those abilities to serve Him more boldly?

5. No Delay in Pursuing an Immediate Goal

David did not procrastinate, make excuses, or stall. He took action.

☜ When have you procrastinated in obeying the Lord? What was the result?

☜ When have you obeyed Him immediately, even though you might have been uncertain of the outcome? How did that obedience strengthen you?

6. Cooperation

David sought the cooperation of others. The battle against the Philistines was not a one-man show. David may have fought Goliath one-on-one, but he did not take on the entire Philistine army single-handedly. Prior to facing Goliath, David had spread his own confidence throughout the Israelite camp. The soldiers were stirred up, ready to take on the battle as soon as David was victorious. The moment David cut off Goliath's head, "the men of Israel and Judah arose and shouted, and pursued the Philistines as far as the entrance to the valley and to the gates of Ekron" (1 Sam. 17:52).

If the Lord has laid a goal on your heart, He is already working to prepare the hearts of others to help you reach that goal. He may be working in you to help another person with a goal that you share. Either way, we ultimately are to work together to spread the gospel, extend the kingdom of God, and build up the body of Christ. Seek out those with whom you can work toward a common goal.

7. Consistency in Pursuing the Goal

David did not lose sight of the big goal of his life, which was to serve God as king of Israel. After defeating Goliath, he took the head of Goliath back to Jerusalem as a signal to all the people that the Lord had delivered them from their enemy. He also took the armor of Goliath into his own tent as a constant reminder of what the Lord had enabled him to do. David knew that in the years ahead he would need to be reminded that God was bigger than any problem he faced. He knew that the Israelites also needed to be encouraged to trust the Lord more.

Don't lose sight of your long-range goals, even as you throw your energies into accomplishing your short-term or immediate goals. Paul encouraged Titus that believers are to "maintain good works" even as they "meet urgent needs." To get caught up in urgent needs and to fail to maintain the overall good works of our life is to be "unfruitful."

And let our people also learn to maintain good works, to meet urgent needs, that they may not be unfruitful.

—Titus 3:14

What does it mean "to maintain good works"? What good works did Paul have in mind? Why do such things need mainte-nance?

When have urgent needs prevented you from more important tasks? How can you prevent urgencies from ruling your life?

8. Emotions Kept Under Control

David could have become frustrated or angry at the opposition that his brothers gave him. He could have become embroiled in arguments with the other soldiers. He could have become discouraged and gone back home. David didn't give in to any of these options. He saved all of his emotional energy for the battle.

As you pursue your God-given goals, make a decision to save your emo-tional energy for those decisions and actions that are truly important for you to reach your goal. There are many things that can and must be overlooked or not blown out of proportion. Keep your focus on God's love, God's call, God's help, God's approval, and God's rewards. He will not disappoint you or fail you if you continue to pursue the goals that He sets for your life with focus and determination.

As we pursue our goals, we each will face situations that can cause us to experience fear. Take charge over fear! Encourage yourself in the Lord. Choose to encourage others around you and to associate with upbeat, faith-filled people who can encourage you daily.

Later in David's life, he faced a defeat. Amalekites entered David's stronghold at Ziklag while David and his men were out of the city, and they set fire to the city and took captive all of the women and children. We read in 1 Samuel 30:6, "Now David was greatly distressed, for the people spoke of stoning him, because the soul of all the people was grieved, every man for his sons and his daughters. But David strengthened himself in the LORD his God."

David encouraged himself in the Lord. He focused on what God was able to do, rather than on what man had done. He asked the Lord whether he should pursue the troops who had done evil to him and his men, and the Lord said, "Pursue." So David and four hundred of his men went in pursuit, and "David recovered all that the Amalekites had carried away" (v. 18). I encourage you to read this entire story in 1 Samuel 30.

> Have I not commanded you? Be strong and of good courage;
> do not be afraid, nor be dismayed, for the LORD your God is
> with you wherever you go.
>
> —Joshua 1:9

❧ Why does God command us not to fear? What are the dangers of fear? How can fear be used as a weapon against us, rather than a defense?

How might David's situation with the Amalekites have ended if he had given in to fear? How did the Philistines use fear to subdue the army of Israel?

9. Courage Developed Over Time

David had courage that had been developed over years and through a variety of experiences. He did not suddenly awaken one morning and have courage to confront Goliath. He had developed courage as a shepherd boy, protecting his father's flocks against the elements and against predatory animals, including a lion and a bear. David no doubt had experienced many moments in which he'd had to stare down his own fears while alone with his flocks in wilderness areas.

Ask the Lord today to give you the daily courage that you need as you face the tasks and temptations before you. Ask Him to give you courage to accomplish the immediate and short-range goals that you have set. That will be your best possible means of developing the courage that you will need when major crises or obstacles arise.

Therefore I remind you to stir up the gift of God which is in you. . . . For God has not given us a spirit of fear, but of power and of love and of a sound mind.

—2 Timothy 1:6, 7

🖎 What role does a "sound mind" play in being courageous? How does one's thinking and attitude build courage? How does it instill unnecessary fear?

🖎 Why did Paul command us to "stir up the gift of God"? In what ways do God's gifts need to be stirred up? How is this done?

10. A Conscious Dependence on God at All Times

Throughout the story of David's battle with Goliath, we find references to the Lord. David had a conscious, openly expressed dependence on God. Let your conversations and your statements to others reflect your dependence upon the Lord. Remember at all times that none of us can accomplish anything of eternal benefit in our own strength.

> I would have lost heart, unless I had believed that I would see the goodness of the LORD in the land of the living. Wait on the LORD; be of good courage, and He shall strengthen your heart; wait, I say, on the LORD!
>
> —Psalm 27:13, 14

What does it mean to "wait on the Lord"? How is this done? How does it build courage?

What enabled David to find the courage that he needed, according to these verses? On what did he build his faith?

Today and Tomorrow

TODAY: GOD HAS COMMANDED ME TO BE COURAGEOUS, SINCE FEAR IS MY ENEMY.

TOMORROW: I WILL ASK THE LORD TO INCREASE MY COURAGE AND HELP ME TO DEFEAT FEAR IN THE COMING WEEK.

LESSON 6

Money and Success

─────── ❧ **In This Lesson** ❧ ───────

LEARNING: HOW CAN I CONSIDER MYSELF SUCCESSFUL WHEN I'M NOT WEALTHY?

GROWING: WHAT ROLE DOES MONEY PLAY IN GOD'S DEFINITION OF SUCCESS?

∽∞∾

One of the greatest deceptions in our nation today is that success equals wealth. Becoming the person that God wants you to be and achieving the goals that He sets for your life are what make a person genuinely successful. Wealth has virtually nothing to do with your becoming the person that God wants you to be. And wealth, solely for the sake of acquiring wealth, is not a goal that God sets for a person's life. You will find no admonition in the Bible for a person to strive to become rich materially.

This does not mean that a rich person cannot be successful in God's eyes, nor does it mean that God never blesses a person with material wealth. It does mean that wealth is not the gauge by which we are to determine success. God has different standards of measurement.

In this lesson, we are going to take a look at what the Bible says about money. (If this topic is of special interest to you, I encourage you to read the study guide in this series entitled *Understanding Financial Stewardship.*)

What the Bible Teaches About Money

The Bible has more verses devoted to finances and money, and to our proper use of them, than to verses about heaven! God knew that money was a practical matter that would require our attention on a daily basis. Money is a vital part of our lives.

For the most part, the Bible regards money as simply a medium of exchange. It is intended to be used for righteous purposes. It is a blessing of God given to us so that we might be stewards of a portion of the Lord's bountiful supply. In many cases, it is a tool that God uses to test our trust and faithfulness. The apostle Paul taught,

> We urge you, brethren, that you increase more and more; that you also aspire to lead a quiet life, to mind your own business, and to work with our own hands, as we commanded you, that you may walk properly toward those who are outside, and that you may lack nothing.

> —1 Thessalonians 4:10–12

These verses have a two-fold message. First, the Lord expects us to work so that we are not in financial or material need. Second, the Lord wants us to *increase more and more.*

⌘ What does it mean, in the world's eyes, to "increase more and more"? What does it mean in God's eyes? What does it mean in your eyes?

☙ Why did Paul command his readers to work with their own hands? In what way did this enable them to "walk properly toward those who are outside"?

Three Key Principles

The Bible has three overriding principles regarding money and material wealth. We are wise to keep them in mind always.

1. God Is the Source of All Blessings.

All wealth comes from God. Anytime we look at what we have in terms of possessions or financial holdings, we should be quick to say, "God is the One who has given me this."

☙ What is your first response when you receive a promotion or an unexpected financial windfall? How does your attitude influence your use of those things?

2. There Is No Lasting Ownership of Anything Material

Even those things that you have bought and paid for will not be yours forever. None of us can take any material blessing from this life into eternity.

For no sooner has the sun risen with a burning heat than it
withers the grass; its flower falls, and its beautiful appearance
perishes. So the rich man also will fade away in his pursuits.

—James 1:11

⁓ In what ways are material possessions like grass on a hot
summer day? Why is it unwise to chase after such things?

⁓ What does God want you to pursue instead? How can money
and possessions interfere with God's priorities for your life?

3. We Are Privileged by God to Use Things to Bless People

God allows certain amounts of wealth and certain possessions to come
into our hands so that we might use them to bring blessing to others.
We are to be a funnel for God's blessings, not a container in which
to hoard them. We must always be determined to use things and love
people, rather than love things and use people!

Command those who are rich in this present age not to be
haughty, nor to trust in uncertain riches but in the living God,
who gives us richly all things to enjoy. Let them do good, that

they be rich in good works, ready to give, willing to share, storing up for themselves a good foundation for the time to come, that they may lay hold on eternal life.

—1 Timothy 6:17–19

∂ Why did Paul specify people who are rich "in this present age"? What does this suggest about the difference between temporal riches and eternal riches?

∂ According to these verses, what is the proper use of material blessings? What are the results of using them wisely?

Five Things that Jesus Taught About Money

Many people conclude that Jesus favored poverty and had very little good to say about wealth. Let's take a closer look at five things that Jesus taught about money.

1. Pursuit of Wealth Must Never Be Our Number-One Priority

Jesus gave us this very solemn warning about a love for money: "For what profit is it to a man if he gains the whole world, and loses his own soul? Or what will a man give in exchange for his soul?" (Matt. 16:26).

Jesus plainly taught that we are to seek first the kingdom of God, and that those who make the acquisition of wealth their top priority will find it very difficult to gain heavenly reward.

> Jesus said to him, "If you want to be perfect, go, sell what you have and give to the poor, and you will have treasure in heaven; and come, follow Me." But when the young man heard that saying, he went away sorrowful, for he had great possessions.
>
> —Matthew 19:21, 22

᙭ This young man had kept the Law of Moses from his youth— but he ended up walking away from Jesus. What did this reveal about his top priorities?

᙭ Why did Jesus require the young man to sell what he had before following Him? How can material wealth interfere with full obedience to Christ?

2. We Err Greatly When We Hoard Our Wealth and Fail to Give Generously to Those in Need

One day a man came to Jesus and said, "Teacher, tell my brother to divide the inheritance with me" (Luke 12:13). Jesus replied,

"Man, who made Me a judge or an arbitrator over you?" And
He said to them, "Take heed and beware of covetousness, for
one's life does not consist in the abundance of things he possesses."

—Luke 12:14, 15

"Do not lay up for yourselves treasures on earth, where moth
and rust destroy and where thieves break in and steal; but lay
up for yourselves treasures in heaven, where neither moth nor
rust destroys and where thieves do not break in and steal. For
where your treasure is, there your heart will be also."

—Matthew 6:19–21

☙ How does a person lay up treasures in heaven? How is the
acquisition of eternal treasure similar to gaining earthly wealth?
How are the two different?

☙ Why does a person's heart tend to be controlled by his possessions? How do possessions tend to turn one away from having a heart for God?

3. Those Who Give Generously to the Lord Will Receive Generously from the Lord

Jesus said, "Give, and it will be given to you: good measure, pressed down, shaken together, and running over will be put into your bosom. For with the same measure that you use, it will be measured back to you" (Luke 6:38). Whatever we give to others, the Lord returns to us in the form of what we need. The Lord gives us precisely what we need, and He gives it in overflowing supply. Furthermore, He very often gives to us through people other than those to whom we have given.

🖎 Why did Jesus say that He will give to us in the same measure that we use when we give to others? What are the implications of this giving and receiving ratio?

🖎 Define what each of the following would be like in a basket of grain, and note how generous each is. What is the result when all are put together?

Good measure:

Pressed down:

Shaken together:

Running over:

4. We Are to Be Faithful Stewards of All That We Have Regardless of How Much We Have?

Jesus said, "He who is faithful in what is least is faithful also in much; and he who is unjust in what is least is unjust also in much. Therefore if you have not been faithful in the unrighteous mammon, who will commit to your trust the true riches? And if you have not been faithful in what is another man's, who will give you what is your own?" (Luke 16:10–12).

When people hear a sermon about tithing or giving, too often they respond, "Well, I'll tithe when I make more money." The sad fact is that they won't. The person who is faithful in tithing one dollar, two dollars, five dollars, and a hundred dollars will be faithful in tithing when he earns much more.

Material wealth is not limited to money or stocks and bonds. Your house or apartment is a form of material wealth. The car that you drive and the things that you own are aspects of your material wealth. When we take good care of the things that the Lord has already given to us, He can entrust us with His greater riches, which include inner riches such as spiritual leadership.

☙ What "true riches" was Jesus speaking of in Luke 16 above? What is "unrighteous mammon"?

∽ Why does God want us to be faithful with material blessings before He entrusts other responsibilities to us?

5. Our Stewardship Is Directly Related to What We Worship or What We Serve

Jesus said, "No servant can serve two masters; for either he will hate the one and love the other, or else he will be loyal to the one and despise the other. You cannot serve God and mammon" (Luke 16:13). The thing that is at the center of your thinking or the center of your desire is the thing that you worship—it is the thing that you serve, the thing that you admire and respect the most, the thing for which you long the most. Those who place financial gain as their top priority in life have given money the place that belongs to God. They are guilty of idolatry.

The greedy person desires the blessing of money more than he desires the Giver of all blessings. He cannot be satisfied and is never truly thankful for what the Lord has given. The more you earn and the more you acquire, the more you need to be in the Word of God, seeking direction and wisdom about how to use the money that the Lord has given to you.

Through my years of ministry, I have seen a number of people prosper in their businesses and acquire small fortunes. Unfortunately, some of these people didn't have any idea how to handle large sums of money, and they lost the fortunes that they had acquired. Others who became increasingly wealthy knew how to handle their money, but they lost sight of God's purposes in giving them money. Rather than use their money to support the work of the Lord and do good, they used their money for their own selfish pleasures. In the end, these people may not have lost their fortunes, but they lost sight of what truly mattered in life. They lost their peace of mind, their joy in the Lord, and their inner sense of fulfillment and satisfaction. They had money, but they were not genuinely successful.

Choose to be wise about money. It is a factor involved in success because it is a factor of our lives as a whole. But it is neither the definition of success nor should it ever be the foremost priority of our lives.

> For the love of money is a root of all kinds of evil, for which some have strayed from the faith in their greediness, and pierced themselves through with many sorrows. But you, O man of God, flee these things and pursue righteousness, godliness, faith, love, patience, gentleness.
>
> —1 Timothy 6:10, 11

🖝 Why are we commanded to flee from the love of money? How is this done, in practical terms?

What is involved in pursuing righteousness and godliness? In pursuing patience and gentleness? Why don't these pursuits allow a person to also pursue wealth?

Today and Tomorrow

TODAY: GOD MIGHT CHOOSE TO BLESS ME WITH WEALTH, BUT THAT MUST NEVER BE MY GOAL IN LIFE.

TOMORROW: I WILL ASK THE LORD TO TEACH ME HOW TO BE FAITHFUL WITH MATERIAL BLESSINGS, SO THAT I MIGHT BECOME FAITHFUL IN ETERNAL BLESSINGS.

LESSON 7

Hurdling the Roadblocks to Success

❧ In This Lesson ❧

LEARNING: BUT WHAT CAN I DO ABOUT [FILL IN THE BLANK] THAT KEEPS ME FROM SUCCEEDING?

GROWING: HOW DO I REMOVE ROADBLOCKS THAT ARE BIGGER THAN I AM?

❧

Why do some people fail to reach their goals? Why does success seem to elude some people who truly want to be successful? A wide variety of reasons have been suggested, but I believe that the root reasons for failing to fulfill God-given goals lie inside a person. They are not external, material, or circumstantial reasons.

Laying Aside Every Weight

Hebrews 12:1, 2 gives us an important insight that can help us overcome the roadblocks that we encounter on our path toward success:

> Therefore we also, since we are surrounded by so great a cloud of witnesses, let lay aside every weight, and the sin which so easily ensnares us, and let us run with endurance the race that is set before us, looking unto Jesus, the author and finisher of our faith, who for the joy that was set before Him endured the cross, despising the shame, and has sat down at the right hand of the throne of God.

74

The good news in this passage is that you are surrounded by a host of encouragers, both those who are living and those who have gone on to be with the Lord. There are countless saints of God who have lived successful lives in Christ Jesus, and they can be a great inspiration to us. Two of the greatest things that you can do for yourself are to read biographies of great Christian men and women, both those in history and those who are alive today, and to associate with older and more mature Christians who are experiencing success God's way.

∾ Who has been a role model or mentor in your life? What qualities in that person's life do you admire? How has he or she influenced your life?

∾ What are the weights that we are called to lay aside in Hebrews 12 above? What sorts of things can be a burden in your life? How are those things laid aside?

The Lord Himself, of course, should always be our greatest encourager. He tells us in Hebrews 13:5, "I will never leave you nor forsake you." The Lord is present with us always to help us, teach us, guide us, comfort us, and empower us. He is the One who gives us the strength and ability to hurdle the roadblocks that lie in our path to success.

∾ *Weights.* Weights are those things that trouble us, weigh heavily on our minds, and cause us to be worried, frustrated, or discouraged.

75

Sins. Sins are those things that entangle us and cause us to miss out on God's blessings and opportunities.

Both are things that we must put down. Nobody else can strip these things from our lives. We must take charge and lay aside those things that hold us back from our pursuit of godly goals. We are the ones who must choose to run with endurance the race that the Lord sets before us.

What sins have entangled you in the past or present? In what sense are they like a net that holds you captive? What is or was required to cut yourself free from those sins?

Seven Roadblocks to Success

In this lesson, we are going to focus on seven roadblocks that keep us back from godly success.

1. The Roadblock of Gripping Fear

A gripping fear paralyzes us with feelings that we are threatened, incapable, or inadequate. It is not a normal, instinctive fear, such as the fear of falling or the fear that suddenly grips us in a dangerous situation. This is fear that keeps us bottled up and stagnant. Gripping fears may cause us to become defensive and look for excuses about why we are not succeeding. These fears can cause us to flee from our goals or to dismiss our goals as being unimportant or invalid.

Faith is the opposite of fear. It is the solution for fear. In order to hurdle this roadblock, you are going to have to do things that build up your faith. The first and best thing that any of us can do to build up our faith is to get our eyes off our problem and off ourselves and onto Jesus. He is the One who is utterly reliable and who possesses all knowledge, authority, power, ability, wisdom, and strength. I encourage you to immerse yourself in reading and memorizing Scriptures that will build up your faith. Anytime a gripping fear takes hold of you, speak aloud faith-building verses. Ask the Lord to manifest the truth of these verses in your life.

> Fear not, for I am with you; be not dismayed, for I am your God. I will strengthen you, yes, I will help you, I will uphold you with My righteous right hand.
>
> —Isaiah 41:10

Why does God command us throughout Scripture not to have fear? In what ways is fear a destructive force? How does a person choose not to be afraid?

What reasons does God give us in this verse to not be afraid? What can His righteous right hand accomplish in your life?

2. The Roadblock of Nagging Doubt

A success roadblock closely related to fear is doubt. Doubt is a lack of assurance. When we doubt, we become unsteady, tentative, and wavering in our pursuit of a goal. We may not become paralyzed or be put into flight mode as with fear, but we may become bogged down and miss important opportunities for advancement.

Hebrews 11:6 tells us, "Without faith it is impossible to please Him, for he who comes to God must believe that He is, and that He is a rewarder of those who diligently seek Him." We please God by receiving His Son, Jesus Christ, as our Savior, and by obeying Him day by day. The exercise of our faith requires daily obedience to what God tells us to do, both in His commandments and in the pursuit of the goals that He has designed for our lives.

One of the main reasons that people doubt is that they lack understanding that God is with them always. Anytime you experience momentary doubt, I encourage you to get on your knees, open your Bible, and begin to read God's Word aloud back to God, saying, "Lord, this is what You have said in Your Word. I am trusting You to do this in my life."

> For we walk by faith, not by sight.
>
> —2 Corinthians 5:7

☙ What does it mean to walk by faith? How is this done? How is this different from walking by sight?

∾ Why is it impossible to walk by sight in the Christian life? What things are revealed by sight? What things are revealed only by faith?

3. The Roadblock of Excuses

Excuse-itis is an infection of self-justifications and excuses that takes root and rots away at a person's desire to pursue godly goals. It is the habit of offering an excuse at every turn for not doing what one knows he should do. It is the cornerstone of the blame game in which we make ourselves feel better about our failure to pursue godly goals, blaming other people, blaming conditions or situations, even blaming our own weaknesses and failures.

Jesus told a parable about a rich man who went on a journey and entrusted his wealth to three servants. To one he gave five talents (a talent is a unit of money), to another two talents, and to a third just one talent. When the master returned, he found that the first two servants had doubled his money in his absence. The third servant, however, got into excuse-itis. He said, "Lord, I knew you to be a hard man, reaping where you have not sown, and gathering where you have not scattered seed. And I was afraid, and went and hid your talent in the ground. Look, there you have what is yours" (Matt. 25:24, 25).

This servant attempted to blame his master for his failure to do anything with the wealth that had been entrusted to him! The master called this servant "wicked and lazy" and took the talent from him and gave it to the one who had produced ten talents.

Never try to blame another person for your failures. Redirect that energy into getting started on the pursuit of your God-given goals. One of the best ways to overcome excuse-itis is to get in involved in an accountability group or relationship. The support and prayers of the others can be an encouragement to you, and they can also provide a reality check for you to keep you from playing the blame game.

> "Then he who had received the one talent came and said, 'Lord, I knew you to be a hard man, reaping where you have not sown, and gathering where you have not scattered seed.'"

> —Matthew 25:24

In Jesus' parable, was the third servant correct in his assessment of his master's character? Did the master demonstrate harshness to his servants, or generosity and trust?

How did this third servant's views of his master lead him into failure? How can your conception of God lead you into either success or failure?

4. The Roadblock of Procrastination

Procrastination is putting off until tomorrow what you know you should do today. Two main types of people are prone to procrastination:

1. Perfectionists. The first type of person prone to procrastination is the perfectionist. The perfectionist is not simply a person who does the best he can at the things he undertakes—the perfectionist feels driven to do everything perfectly. The perfectionist, therefore, often procrastinates from undertaking projects because he anticipates the possibility of failure or the inevitability of falling short of perfection.

2. Discomfort-dodgers. The second type of person prone to procrastination is the discomfort-dodger. This person knows that accomplishing goals takes effort, energy, and saying no to frivolous pleasures and fleshly lusts—all of which are the opposite of a life of ease.

If you are a perfectionist or a discomfort-dodger, ask the Lord to help you overcome these detrimental traits. The fact is, nobody is perfect except God. God knows all about your imperfections and still chooses to reside in you by the power of the Holy Spirit, who helps you overcome your imperfections. The perfecting work is His, not yours. God will help you to overcome emotional laziness, but you must do the work of motivating yourself and choosing to expend energy and effort. God will do for you what you cannot do, but not what you *choose* not to do.

One of the best ways to overcome procrastination is to set a limited number of very specific, obtainable daily goals. Write them down, and every morning ask the Lord to help you accomplish the things that you have identified on your list.

See then that you walk circumspectly, not as fools but as wise, redeeming the time, because the days are evil.

—Ephesians 5:15, 16

∾ What does it mean to walk circumspectly? Give some practical examples.

∾ What does it mean to be "redeeming the time"? How is this done? Why is it essential to redeem time if "the days are evil"?

5. The Roadblock of Insatiable Greed

Greed is an insatiable craving for acquiring more than a person needs. It has no bottom to it: it can never be satisfied, and nothing is ever enough. Greed grows from having one's focus on the things of this world. It causes a person to want more and more of what is material and financial. The greedy person pursues just one more dollar, one more acquisition, one more fix or pill, one more piece of property. The

82

more a person pursues that one more thing, the less he has eyes for true spiritual concerns and riches.

The pursuit of the natural world eventually supersedes all desire to pursue the things of God. When that happens, a person's life falls out of balance, and God-given goals take a backseat. No person who is bound by the natural world can be truly successful in God's eyes. The Lord's desire is always that we hunger and thirst for those things that He establishes as good for us and for others around us.

Furthermore, there is no way that a greedy person can practice greed without stepping on somebody's toes or alienating other people. The greedy person tends to wall off other people whom he perceives as being in competition for what he desires. The greedy person also tends to abuse and take advantage of other people in his unending quest to put more and more worldly good under his control. One of the best remedies for greed is to begin to give sacrificially—to give away a possession that you value highly or to give to the degree that you eliminate a luxury.

> Therefore put to death your members which are on the earth: fornication, uncleanness, passion, evil desire, and covetousness, which is idolatry.
>
> —Colossians 3:5

᳹ In what sense is covetousness at the root of greed? How are greed and covetousness the same as idolatry?

☞ What does it mean to put greed to death? How is this done? Why is it so important to do so?

6. The Roadblock of Sin

Another way of stating this roadblock is "the violation of conscience." Your conscience acts as an internal alarm system in your spirit and soul that you have entered into a sin zone. Your conscience warns you against dangers that can lead to moral and spiritual destruction.

The more a person violates his conscience, the less sensitive his conscience becomes. His understanding of what is right and wrong becomes cloudy and uncertain. His ability to discern evil becomes inoperative. Such a person is more prone to embark on detours that can lead him away from genuine success.

> Now the Spirit expressly says that in latter times some will depart from the faith, giving heed to deceiving spirits and doctrines of demons, speaking lies in hypocrisy, having their own conscience seared with a hot iron.
>
> —1 Timothy 4:1, 2

≈ How does habitual sin cause a person's conscience to become seared, as with hot iron? What is the result of a seared conscience?

≈ How can a seared conscience be renewed? What role does the Holy Spirit play in that process? What role does a person play?

7. The Roadblock of Slothfulness

In the Bible, being slothful or lazy is contrasted to being industrious and working diligently. The slothful person does as little as possible and seeks to get by in life with minimal effort, minimal expenditure of creativity and energy, and minimal involvement with others. None of these behaviors is associated with godly success! The pursuit of godly goals takes energy. Building godly relationships takes diligence and effort. The pursuit of godly success takes an expenditure of time and creativity.

If you struggle with slothfulness, I encourage you to reevaluate your goals. Perhaps you haven't identified goals that have a sense of God-given urgency about them. Perhaps you haven't identified goals toward which you feel a strong compulsion to act. Set goals that motivate you, and then insist within yourself that you will get up each morning and pursue them to the best of your ability.

He who is slothful in his work is a brother to him who is a great destroyer.

—Proverbs 18:9

In what sense is a lazy person the brother of those who destroy? What sorts of things are destroyed by those who are habitually lazy?

What is the solution to laziness? What role does the Holy Spirit play in that process? What role does a person play?

Keeping Your Sights on the Future Ahead

Never let a roadblock cloud your ultimate vision of godly success. Don't allow yourself to become so immersed in solving an immediate problem or overcoming an immediate obstacle that you lose sight of the big picture of your most important goals. Ask the Lord to help you keep your focus on Him and on what He wants you to be and do in your life.

Ask the Holy Spirit to help you as you take action to remove these road-blocks to your success. The Holy Spirit will not override your personal will or sovereignly remove these weights and sins from your path, but when you invite Him to help you, He will do so!

List below the roadblocks in your life and what you will do this week to start removing them.

Roadblock	What I'll Do This Week

Today and Tomorrow

TODAY: GOD WILL GIVE ME HIS SPIRIT TO HELP ME MOVE THE MOST DAUNTING OBSTACLES IN MY LIFE.

TOMORROW: I WILL FULFILL THE ACTION PLAN THIS WEEK WHICH I HAVE OUTLINED IN THE TABLE ABOVE.

LESSON 8

Successful Attitudes and Ideas

---- ⚞ **In This Lesson** ⚟ ----

LEARNING: WHAT IS THE TRUTH ABOUT GOD'S CHARACTER?

GROWING: HOW DOES MY THOUGHT LIFE INFLUENCE MY SUCCESS?

Have you ever stopped to think that everything around you first began with a thought? It either began as a thought in the mind of God or as a thought in the mind of a man. What an awesome, creative power lies in our minds, the organ of thinking and the seat of opinions and attitudes. Few of us ever stop to consider the power of our own thoughts and attitudes, but the Bible proclaims about a man, "As he thinks in his heart, so is he" (Prov. 23:7).

In order to become the person that God wants us to be, we must learn to think as Jesus thinks. The apostle Paul wrote, "Let this mind be in you which was also in Christ Jesus" (Phil. 2:5). The Bible is very specific about the thought life that we are to have as believers—the thought life that leads to our being what He created us to be.

Finally, brethren, whatever things are true, whatever things are noble, whatever things are just, whatever things are pure, whatever things are lovely, whatever things are of good report, if there is any virtue and if there is anything praiseworthy—meditate on these things.

—Philippians 4:8

☙ Define the following in your own words, giving practical examples of each.

Noble:

Just:

Pure:

Lovely:

Good report:

Monitoring Your Own Thought Life

There are four main areas of your thought life that are important for you to monitor diligently.

1. What Are You Thinking About Yourself?

How you think or feel about yourself is going to be projected into the way that you behave, including the choices that you make and the way that you approach problems. A negative perception will manifest itself in your speech, usually in the form of criticism and negative comments. It will manifest itself in your body language, perhaps in the form of a limp handshake, a slouchy walk, a drooped head, downcast eyes, or a sad expression. It will manifest itself in the way that you work—if you don't value yourself, you are more likely to produce less work or lower quality.

When you change the way that you think about yourself, very often you change the way that others think about you, and that, in turn, often changes the circumstances and situations in which you find yourself.

> I will praise You, for I am fearfully and wonderfully made; marvelous are Your works, and that my soul knows very well. My frame was not hidden from You, when I was made in secret, and skillfully wrought in the lowest parts of the earth. Your eyes saw my substance, being yet unformed. And in Your book they all were written, the days fashioned for me, when as yet there were none of them.
>
> —Psalm 139:14–16

∽ What does the Psalmist mean by saying that your days were all written and fashioned for you before your birth? What does this suggest about God's view of you?

∽ If you were skillfully and wonderfully made by God Himself, what does this suggest about your inherent abilities? About your value within the body of Christ?

2. What Are You Thinking About Your Circumstances?

How do you feel about your home, your place of employment, or your neighborhood? The way that you think and feel about your environment is going to affect the ways that you behave, treat your possessions, schedule your time, manage your money, and communicate with others who share your home, workplace, or community. Your perceptions about your environment will influence your perceptions about your own potential for success.

☙ Read Numbers 13. What does it mean that the promised land was flowing with milk and honey? How would you describe such a place?

☙ Why did Joshua and Caleb encourage the Israelites to boldly enter the promised land, as God had commanded them to do?

☙ Why did the other ten spies discourage the Israelites from entering the promised land? What effect did their attitude have on the nation as a whole?

3. What Are You Thinking About Other People?

Are there certain classes or groups of people that you don't like in general? Your thoughts and feelings about other people determine your relationships. People tend to cluster around commonly held beliefs or a mutually held perspective on life. To a great extent, what you think influences your choice of friends, spouse, business associates, and mentors. All of these key relationships, in turn, affect your progress toward the goals that God has set for your life. Especially consider the thoughts and feelings that you have toward your family and children. Do you see them as a gift of God to your life?

> Let nothing be done through selfish ambition or conceit, but in lowliness of mind let each esteem others better than himself. Let each of you look out not only for his own interests, but also for the interests of others.
>
> —Philippians 2:3, 4

Define "lowliness of mind." How is this different from harboring feelings of inferiority? How do these verses influence correct thinking about yourself?

If you changed your thinking about the people in your life as Paul commands, how might it affect your attitudes toward your home? Toward work? Toward church?

4. What Do You Think About God?

Your relationship with God will be influenced by how well you understand His character. If you think of God as a judge who is keeping score continually about your behavior and judging you guilty and unworthy at every turn, you are far less likely to want to spend time with Him in prayer or to meditate on His Word. On the other hand, if you think of God as a loving Father, you are much more likely to spend time reading His Word and communicating with Him.

The sad irony of this is that a Christian needs to be spending time daily in God's Word if he is to gain an accurate understanding of God's character. Faulty thinking about who God is can actually prevent you from doing the one thing that will correct that faulty thinking: spending time in His presence in prayer and meditation on Scriptures. Your thoughts about God will directly affect your faith.

> Hear, O Israel: The LORD our God, the LORD is one! You shall love the LORD your God with all your heart, with all your soul, and with all your strength. And these words which I command you today shall be in your heart.
>
> —Deuteronomy 6:4–6

Read Deuteronomy 6 for context on these verses. What role does God's Word play in understanding who God is, according to the chapter?

☙ Why is it vitally important to have an accurate understanding of God? What areas of your life are influenced by your understanding of God?

God's Challenge to Think Positively

A negative response is never warranted to the life that God sets before us. Of all the people that we encounter in the New Testament, the apostle Paul probably had the greatest reason to develop negative thinking. He encountered a host of negative situations and responses to his preaching of the gospel. The last years of his life were spent in confinement. Even so, read what Paul wrote to the Philippians from his prison chamber in Rome:

> But I rejoiced in the Lord greatly that now at last your care for me has flourished again; though you surely did care, but you lacked opportunity. Not that I speak in regard to need, for I have learned in whatever state I am, to be content: I know how to be abased, and I know how to abound. Everywhere and in all things I have learned both to be full and to be hungry, both to abound and to suffer need. I can do all things through Christ who strengthens me . . . I am full, having received from Epaphroditus the things sent from you, a sweet-smelling aroma, an acceptable sacrifice, well pleasing to God. And my God shall supply all your need according to His riches in glory by Christ Jesus.
>
> —Philippians 4:10–13, 18, 19

Even though he was in prison, Paul wrote with an attitude of thanksgiving, encouragement, contentment, and faith in the Lord to supply his needs and the needs of the Philippians. Paul was a man who chose to think *God's* way—that adversity does not mean defeat—and to believe in God's highest and best at all times. He chose to remain positive and hopeful about his future and the future of others.

Paul was not an idealist or a fantasizer. He was a realist. He didn't deny that he faced problems or that he was in prison. Paul recognized, however, as we must, that life is never totally negative or totally positive. We can choose which side of life to think about and focus on.

☙ Why did Paul say above that he had learned to be content? How is contentment learned? Why is it a skill, rather than something dependent upon circumstances?

☙ What did Paul mean when he said, "I can do all things through Christ who strengthens me"? What things was he referring to?

Lining Up Our Thinking with God's Word

Each of us is challenged to line up our thinking and our attitudes with God's Word. Many have been programmed to think and to respond to life in ways that are contrary to God's best. Paul wrote to the Romans:

> I beseech you therefore, brethren, by the mercies of God, that you present your bodies a living sacrifice, holy, acceptable to God, which is your reasonable service. And do not be conformed to this world, but be transformed by the renewing of your mind, that you may prove what is that good and acceptable and perfect will of God.
>
> —Romans 12:1, 2

The transformation of our minds to be conformed to the things of God is our responsibility, nobody else's. The word for *renewing* the mind means "to make a change." We must choose to change the way that we think so that our thoughts and feelings are in line with God's truth.

> Your word I have hidden in my heart, That I might not sin against You.
>
> —Psalm 119:11

⚞ What does it mean to hide God's Word in your heart? How is this done?

In what ways does God's Word prevent a person from sinning? How does a correct understanding of His character prevent sin?

 Today and Tomorrow

TODAY: A CORRECT UNDERSTANDING OF GOD IS ESSENTIAL IN BECOMING SUCCESSFUL.

TOMORROW: I WILL SPEND TIME IN PRAYER AND SCRIPTURE STUDY EACH DAY THIS WEEK.

LESSON 9

A Successful Use of Time

✎ In This Lesson ✐

LEARNING: WHAT DOES MY USE OF TIME HAVE TO DO WITH SUCCESS?

GROWING: HOW DO I BALANCE PLANNING WITH WALKING BY FAITH?

Success cannot be separated from a wise use of time. Many people attempt to be successful without any thought to time, but those who attain success have learned to respect and honor time in their lives. The apostle Paul had this to say about time management:

> See then that you walk circumspectly, not as fools but as wise, redeeming the time, because the days are evil.
>
> —Ephesians 5:15, 16

To "walk circumspectly" is to be careful in the way that one lives. It is to live an intentional life—not following every whim, but pursuing a course in life that is purposeful. It is to recognize that moments are important.

To the Galatians, Paul wrote, "Let us not grow weary while doing good . . . as we have opportunity, let us do good to all" (Gal. 6:9, 10). The word for *opportunity* means "making the most of your time." Time and opportunity are vitally linked to success.

Why does Paul say that "the days are evil"? In what ways is redeeming time a way of defeating evil?

Circumspection literally means "to see around." Give practical examples of living with circumspection. How does this enable a person to redeem time?

Time Is a Gift from God

God has given each of us a length of time on earth in which to fulfill His plan and purpose for us. Time is a gift to us. Our time on earth is an unknown quantity. We cannot regain lost moments or relive hours. It is up to each of us to ask the Lord, "How can I use my talents and gifts from You in the time that you are giving to me in order to best fulfill Your purpose?"

An Urgency About Time

Throughout the Bible, we find references to the brevity of life and the swift movement of our lives through time. Rather than be discouraged about the brevity of the time we have on earth, we should be all the more eager to make the most of every moment.

> All flesh is grass, and all its loveliness is like the flower of the field. The grass withers, the flower fades, because the breath of the LORD blows upon it; surely the people are grass. The grass withers, the flower fades, but the word of our God stands forever.
>
> —Isaiah 40:6–8

How is life similar to the picture of grass in these verses? What causes the grass to fade away in these verses? How does that picture apply to life?

According to these verses, what is the one thing that never changes? How can this be used to further your success?

A Call to Manage Time Wisely

The Lord expects us to manage our time wisely: creating a balance between work and rest, setting aside times for family and for being with Him, and making prayer and Bible reading a priority in our daily schedules. No person is asked to be a workaholic. To lead a nonstop work life is to live in disobedience to God's commandment: "Six days you shall labor and do all your work, but the seventh day is the Sabbath of the LORD your God" (Ex. 20:9, 10).

Nothing is a waste of time if it is part of a balanced plan for time— a plan that is developed for the fulfillment of God's purposes and for maximum usefulness, productivity, and efficiency in the use of one's talents and gifts.

Five Keys to Good Time Management

The Bible gives us five important and practical principles for good time management:

1. Seek God's Guidance

God has ordained a series of good works for you to accomplish. Ask the Lord each morning to help you identify the good works that He has planned for you on that particular day. Ask the Lord to show you *how* and *when* and to *whom* you might minister by using the good gifts and talents that He has given you.

> For we are His workmanship, created in Christ Jesus for good works, which God prepared beforehand that we should walk in them.
>
> —Ephesians 2:10

❧ What does it mean that God "prepared beforehand" the good works that He wants you to accomplish?

❧ How can you discover what those good works are?

2. Plan Your Schedule

Months can go by without your making any progress toward the fulfill-ment of your God-given goals if you don't plan your schedule and set your God-given goals into the context of deadlines. Ask the Lord to show you how to set your schedule for any given day, week, or year to permit a good balance of work and rest, alone time and family time, input and output.

As we make plans, we must always remain flexible to specific ways in which the Lord may redirect our paths. James said,

> Come now, you who say, "Today or tomorrow we will go to such and such a city, spend a year there, buy and sell, and make a profit"; whereas you do not know what will happen tomorrow. For what is your life? It is even a vapor that appears for a little time and then vanishes away. Instead you ought to say, "If the Lord wills, we shall live and do this or that."

—James 4:13–15

How do these verses apply to making plans for the future? To making decisions for today?

In what ways can advance planning lead to success? In what ways can it lead to failure? What is the key ingredient to planning, according to these verses?

3. Stay Organized

Continually searching for missing documents or items is a waste of time. Stay organized as you work. Throughout the Bible, we find numerous references to doing things and maintaining things in an orderly fashion. (See Exodus 40:1–16, for example.) Organization is a key to efficiency, and efficiency is an important ingredient related to the rate of progress that you can make toward achieving your God-given goals.

Consider what happens to a flock of sheep when no shepherd is present to organize them and keep them together in an orderly fashion:

> They were scattered because there was no shepherd; and they became food for all the beasts of the field when they were scattered.
>
> —Ezekiel 34:5

A similar thing happens to us when we fail to organize the tasks, events, and projects that are put into our care. A lack of organization can lead to loss, struggle, and emotional turmoil.

🖎 When have you wasted a large chunk of time trying to find something that you'd misplaced? What lessons did you learn from that experience?

☜ In what sense is disorganization like a flock of sheep without a shepherd? How can chaos make a person fall prey to the enemy?

4. Eliminate the Unimportant

Many things are not worthy of your time. Let them go! Other things are vitally important to your purpose on the earth. Emphasize them! I am absolutely convinced that, if a person will choose to lay aside all those things that result in a detour from the main purpose that God has for his life, that person will be highly productive, more efficient, and very successful. The Lord spoke to Joshua concerning His Word: "Do not turn from it to the right hand or to the left, that you may prosper wherever you go" (Josh. 1:7). Stay focused in your use of time and your pursuit of your goals!

☜ What does it mean to turn to the right hand or left hand from God's Word? How does this happen? What results?

How can you know when you are in danger of turning away from God's definition of success? What can you do to guard against this?

5. Review Each Day

At the close of a day, review the way in which you have spent your time. Evaluate your schedule. Compare what you did with what you intended to do. Ask yourself:

Did I make good use of my time?
Did I procrastinate?
Was I able to maintain concentration?
Did I engage in activities that were priorities?
Did I make progress toward the accomplishment of my God-given goals?

Now therefore, thus says the LORD of hosts: "Consider your ways! You have sown much, and bring in little; you eat, but do not have enough; you drink, but you are not filled with drink; you clothe yourselves, but no one is warm; and he who earns wages, earns wages to put into a bag with holes." Thus says the LORD of hosts: "Consider your ways!"

—Haggai 1:5–7

☙ What is involved in considering one's ways? How often should one do this?

☙ Read all of Haggai 1. What is God's solution to the problem that the people are facing in their priorities?

A Disciplined, Diligent Life Leads to Success

Ultimately, the wise use of time is a mark of a disciplined life, and a disciplined life, focused on godly goals, results in success. In the Bible, a disciplined life is often called a "diligent life." As you put these five principles of good time management into action on a daily, consistent basis, you are going to discover that you are moving closer and closer to the fulfillment of God's purpose for your life. You will be doing what the Lord has set before you, and you will be in the process of becoming the disciplined person that the Lord wants you to be.

He who has a slack hand becomes poor, but the hand of the diligent makes rich.

—Proverbs 10:4

The hand of the diligent will rule, but the lazy man will be put to forced labor.

—Proverbs 12:24

The soul of a lazy man desires, and has nothing; but the soul of the diligent shall be made rich.

—Proverbs 13:4

The plans of the diligent lead surely to plenty, but those of everyone who is hasty, surely to poverty.

—Proverbs 21:5

᜞ List below some of the benefits of diligence.

List below what is required to become diligent.

❧ Today and Tomorrow ❧

TODAY: THE LORD WANTS ME TO BE DISCIPLINED AND DILIGENT IN MY SERVICE TO HIM.

TOMORROW: I WILL CLOSE EACH DAY THIS WEEK WITH A REVIEW OF HOW I SPENT MY TIME.

Lesson 10

Persisting Until You Succeed

--- ✒ **In This Lesson** ✒ ---

Learning: What happens when I fail?

Growing: How does a person learn to be persistent?

I have never met a person who didn't want to succeed at something. At the same time, I have met very few people who are succeeding at everything—or even most things. Most people seem to allow something, or someone, to deter them, disappoint them, dissuade them, or discourage them from persisting in the pursuit of their goals.

God's plan and purpose for you is always growing. You will never fully arrive at all you can be; you will never do all that you are capable of doing. But each day we are to press toward becoming what God sets out as the character pattern for our lives: the fullness of the maturity of Christ Jesus. We are to continue to endure in our faith toward the goals that God has put before us. There is no justification in God's Word for giving up.

Persistence is the one trait that you are going to find in the life of every person who has achieved something worthwhile in life. It is a combination of strong desire and willpower. It is the capacity to continue on course in the face of all types of difficulties, obstacles, and problems—

without quitting. Persistence is raw determination to move forward rather than to stop or slide backward.

🔊 When has sheer persistence paid off in your life? In the life of someone that you know?

🔊 How does a person cultivate the skill of persistence? What areas of your life require persistence at present?

Is Quitting Ever Justified?

There is never a good enough reason to quit persisting in the pursuit of your goals. The apostle Paul wrote:

> Are they ministers of Christ? . . . I am more: in labors more abundant, in stripes above measure, in prisons more frequent-ly, in deaths often. From the Jews five times I received forty stripes minus one. Three times I was beaten with rods; once I

was stoned; three times I was shipwrecked; a night and a day I have been in the deep; in journeys often, in perils of waters, in perils of robbers, in perils of my own countrymen, in perils of the Gentiles, in perils in the city, in perils in the wilderness, in perils in the sea, in perils among false brethren; in weariness and toil, in sleeplessness often, in hunger and thirst, in fastings often, in cold and nakedness—besides the other things, what comes upon me daily: my deep concern for all the churches.

—2 Corinthians 11:23–28

Is there any person alive today who has gone through so much hardship, pain, and difficulty in the pursuit of his goal? If anybody had a justifiable reason to give up, Paul did. Yet there's no indication in any of his letters that Paul ever quit pressing toward his goals. God calls us to pursue our goals regardless of outer circumstances.

☙ Have you, or someone you know, ever experienced any of the hardships that Paul lists in the verses above?

☙ Note Paul's repetition of "perils." What perils do you face at present? What forces or circumstances require your persistence?

Factors That Affect Persistence

Several factors affect how persistent we will be in pursuing godly success:

   ❧ Focus: Our goals must be well-defined.
   ❧ God-given: We must be certain that God has helped us set our goals.
   ❧ High value: We must see great value in accomplishing our goals, either for ourselves or for the benefit of others.
   ❧ Love factor: When our goals are directly related to someone that we love and want to help, we are much more likely to persist in them.

Jesus gave several parables in which persistence was a key factor:

> What man of you, having a hundred sheep, if he loses one of them, does not leave the ninety-nine in the wilderness, and go after the one which is lost until he finds it? And when he has found it, he lays it on his shoulders, rejoicing . . . Or what woman, having ten silver coins, if she loses one coin, does not light a lamp, sweep the house, and search carefully until she finds it? . . . Likewise, I say to you, there is joy in the presence of the angels of God over one sinner who repents.
>
> —Luke 15:4, 5, 8, 10

❧ Which of the four factors listed above can be found in this parable?

How did Jesus' life demonstrate persistence? How has God shown persistence in His involvement in your life?

No allowances are made in Scripture for quitting due to circumstances or retirement. We are to continue to pursue God's goals for our lives every day of our lives, regardless of external factors.

> Now it came to pass, when the time had come for Him to be received up, that He steadfastly set His face to go to Jerusalem.
>
> —Luke 9:51

What does it mean that Jesus "steadfastly set His face"? What was involved in doing that?

What would have happened if Jesus had quit when His life was threatened? How can His persistence be an example for you this week?

What About Striving?

There are those who claim that we are to cease all striving and to rest in the Lord (see Ps. 46:10; 37:7). But these admonitions do not mean that we are not to persist or to press on with diligence and steadfastness. These verses about resting in the Lord are related to putting our trust in the Lord. We are to rest in Him completely, trusting Him with our whole heart. Jesus did not struggle and strive to make things happen. He trusted the Father. But He did continue to pursue the Father's goals for His life—all the way to the Cross.

> You therefore, beloved, since you know this beforehand, beware lest you also fall from your own steadfastness, being led away with the error of the wicked; but grow in the grace and knowledge of our Lord and Savior Jesus Christ.
>
> —2 Peter 3:17, 18

☙ Being steadfast means to stand firm. What "errors of the wicked" can lead a Christian to fall from being steadfast?

☙ How does a Christian grow in the grace of Christ? How does he grow in knowledge? What will you do this week to accomplish these goals?

Why Persistence Is Required

Persistence is required if we are going to overcome certain things that come into the life of every person from time to time:

&o *Discouragement.* We must persist in pursuing God's success for us even when we don't see much being accomplished, or when our efforts seem futile.

&o *Failures and Mistakes.* All of us fail and make mistakes from time to time. We live in a fallen world, and there's no getting away from the inevitability of error. We must learn from our failures and move on, determined to act more wisely in the future.

&o *Weariness*. We must persist even when we become physically and emotionally tired. Take a rest, but don't quit!

Recall experiences in which you felt discouraged, failed, or felt weary. What did you do to renew your motivation to pursue your goals in life?

Five Principles Related to Persistence

We must always keep in mind several principles that pertain to persistence:

1. A person is not a failure just because he fails. The difference between success and failure is this: The successful person keeps getting up each time he is knocked down. You aren't a failure until you give up.

☙ Recall an experience in which you initially failed, but were later successful.

2. A test does not mean that we are to stop pursuing a goal. A test is an opportunity to learn a valuable lesson on your way to reaching your goals. It is not a stop sign, but very often a "yield more to the Lord" sign, a caution sign, or a "return to the main road" sign.

3. In every failure, you'll find a seed of equivalent success. Choose to learn something from every mistake that you make. Some of the most valuable lessons that you will learn in life relate to what doesn't work or what not to do.

My brethren, count it all joy when you fall into various trials, knowing that the testing of your faith produces patience. But let patience have its perfect work, that you may be perfect and complete, lacking nothing.

—James 1:2–4

∽ What does it mean to "let patience have its perfect work"? What is the perfect work accomplished by patience? How is this process done, in practical terms?

∽ What does James mean when he calls us to "count it all joy" when trials come? How is this done? How is this different from pretending that everything is fine?

4. Bury your failures. Don't keep revisiting your failures with remorse. Bury them and move on. If forgiveness is required, ask God to forgive you and ask others to forgive you. But then forgive yourself and get busy again in the pursuit of your God-given goals.

5. Be quick to forgive others. A person can get so caught up in the blame game or in scheming revenge that he loses all momentum in the pursuit of his goals. We are responsible for our own actions, responses, and feelings, and there is never any justification in God's Word for hurting someone else, harboring unforgiveness, or taking vengeance in our own hands. Ultimately, the blame game hurts us more than it hurts others.

> For if you forgive men their trespasses, your heavenly Father will also forgive you. But if you do not forgive men their trespasses, neither will your Father forgive your trespasses.

> —Matthew 6:14, 15

Why is it vitally important that we forgive others? What is the result of an unforgiving spirit?

Is there someone in your life that you have not forgiven? Take time right now in prayer, telling the Lord that you forgive that person for the specific trespasses.

Keep Your Eyes on the Goal

Periodically revisit your goals. Recall the reasons that your goals were important to you and to God. Rekindle your passion for reaching your God-given goals. Refuse to listen to negative criticism. Good advice is highly valuable when it is rooted in a desire to see you succeed with as few errors as possible. But criticism should never be needed—tearing down your ideas, diminishing the value of your goal, or thwarting a good cause. Listen to what God says about you.

Surround yourself with people who will encourage you. You'll find it much easier to persist in the pursuit of your goals if you are surrounded by people who are encouraging you onward and who believe, as you do, that God is with you and that He will help you.

Remember always that God never gives up on you. He does not waver from His purposes and plans. Paul wrote to the Philippians, "He who has begun a good work in you will complete it until the day of Jesus Christ" (Phil. 1:6). God is never going to give up on the perfecting work that He has started in you.

Did God give up on you when you were a sinner? No. Did God give up on you when you blew it and failed in your witness? No. Did God give up on you when you strayed from Him and began to pursue your own desires and lusts? No. Did God give up on you when you gave up in discouragement on the goals that He gave you? No. Will God ever give up on you? No!

God is always ready and eager to help you begin again, to start over, and to make another attempt. Turn to Him and receive the help that He so generously offers.

Well-Ordered Steps

One of the most important marks of Christian maturity is a continual recognition that the Lord is the One who makes possible all good things in our lives. It is the mature believer who proclaims in all circumstances, "Every good and perfect gift comes from the Father" (see James 1:17).

Even when things seem dark, times are tough, or life seems unsettled, we can know with assurance that God is in charge of our lives and He is working all things together for our good. The Bible tells us,

> The steps of a good man are ordered by the Lord, and He delights in his way.

> —Psalm 37:23

In good times and bad, on mediocre days and exhilarating days, in periods of joy and periods of heavy toil, our stance before the Lord must be, "God, You're in charge. I have no success other than what You help me achieve."

Trust God today to order each step that you take toward the success that He desires for you. Trust Him to order your steps and arrange all the details of your journey as you walk in faith. If you are walking along God's chosen path for you, and you are trusting Him to order each step, you will experience success—God's way!

> The steps of a good man are ordered by the Lord, and He delights in his way. Though he fall, he shall not be utterly cast down; for the Lord upholds him with His hand.

> —Psalm 37:23, 24

☙ What is the definition of a "good man"? What does it mean that his steps are ordered by the Lord? How does a person become good in God's eyes?

☙ Why does the Lord take delight in the way of a good man?

☙ How can a man fall yet still be good in God's eyes? How can this principle encourage you this week in your pursuit of God's plan for success?

᥌ Today and Tomorrow ᥍

TODAY: GOD KNOWS THAT I AM NOT PERFECT, AND HE IS ALWAYS READY TO HELP ME WHEN I FAIL.

TOMORROW: I WILL CONTINUE TO STRIVE TOWARD GOD'S PLAN OF SUCCESS, EVEN WHEN I FACE TRIALS OR FAILURE.

᥌ Notes and Prayer Requests: ᥍

The Life Principles Series

STUDY GUIDES

Other Books by Charles Stanley